T0312911

Hopeful Buildings

Hopeful Buildings

Charles Alexander

Chax Press
Tucson
1990

Sections from "A Book of Hours" appeared in *Ironwood* and *Paper Air*.
The entire poem was published as an artist's book by the 5 & Dime
Press.
"Hopeful Buildings" appeared in *Ottotole*.
"At Text" and "Next a Reading Mine" appeared in *Ironwood*.
"Remains" appeared in *The Sonora Review*.

Thanks to the editors of those magazines and presses, including Michael
Cuddihy, Gil Ott, Michael Amnasan, Lisa Cooper, Michael
Magoolaghan, Penny McElroy, and William Marsh.

Thanks to Lewis Lansford for the typesetting of this manuscript.

Chax Press, 101 West Sixth Street, no. 4, Tucson, Arizona 85701

ISBN 0-925904-03-1
Library of Congress Cataloging-in-Publication Data

Alexander, Charles, 1954–
    Hopeful buildings / by Charles Alexander.
    p.   cm
    Poems.
    ISBN 0-925904-03-1 : $9.95
    I. Title.
PS3551.L3486H6   1990
811'.54--dc20
                                                                90-1405
                                                                CIP

for Cynthia and Kate and Meryle

Contents

A Book of Hours

Foreword / Questions of Hours

> "Beginning again and again and again
> explaining composition and time is a natural
> thing."

Gertrude Stein, "Composition as Explanation"

What is an Hour?

Say an hour is sixty minutes, but that is a division not a definition what is an hour? An hour is a period of time and how one fills it. One fills it. An hour is what we say it is. It is. Let the hours come. Let the hours be filled. Let the hours come again.

> "It was part of it before. And now. There is a
> little more. And so there is more than before.
> Water comes before butter."
>
> "One thoroughly two thoroughly three throughly.
> Three is after all. They were there after all."
>
> Gertrude Stein, *How to Write*

We anticipate the birth of a child.
Water is before.
The subsequent appearance of children has successfully been
       predicted.
Force of love love of force.
One gives one takes away.
Love forces love permits anything to give way to occur.
Force loves nothing impropriety loves propriety.
Green meadows occupy one's attention and one's bare feet.
Love is before one can not live without it.
Don't force me, please.
Eat your Brussels sprouts.
Commands victimize by force imperatives love kind requests.
The face of the moon resembles Chagall's horse.
It is midnight we consider midnight the birth of a child.

He sent his word, and healed them.

And what is knowing, asked the faithful?
Beware not the water.
They began a farm with six used ewes.
Each night, at midnight, look to the moon.
Love encompasses all forces.

Praising the Air / Dialogos

First Attempt Toward Laud

> "to dream takes no effort
>   to think is easy
>   to act is more difficult
>   but for a man to act after he has taken thought, this!
>   is the most difficult thing of all"

Charles Olson, *The Praises*

have faith
fifth later
the intervals
not diminished
make load
stones disappear
and rise
to act
after taking
thought, the
difficulties stand
and wait

do not
praise me
wait third
notes struck
oppose that
sound not
full no

nothing that
way comes
turn the
face upside
up not
down the
door opens
out from
paradise crawls
at midnight
or six
morning I
awakes and
takes shape
time thinking
it all
up again
raises milk
and toast
act fruit
sing bread
forsake nothing

find color

Prime / the First Age

> "Surprised by his use of words, the moral presence
> swelled to veracity plunging the social salad into
> the contemporary fork."
>
> "Though though and though."
>
> Carla Harryman, *Property*

Surprise, the first is not the first,
the last, it continues, first,
and we dine sumptuously.

I have rented a room with champagne
and berries, a pool nearby,
children within audible distance.

Each act of love is renewal
and renovation; to renovate a species
renew lives; we desire to desire.

As pleasing as pancakes in the morning,
if you please, you please me
oh so well, may I please you?

Though night be calm,
though days be long,
though pleasure includes a horse with corral with unfastened
gate.

She stays, and so do you, and so do I.
Change the music tomorrow
we can travel anywhere.

"It is an old religion that put us in our places"

"Behind God's eyes
There might
Be other lights"

Mina Loy, *The Last Lunar Baedeker*

Everything. To say it this way
makes of everything a lump.
A lump is difficult to get round.
A lump is not very interesting.
May we divide it into sections?
We may, a child even may do so.
The one for whom we are waiting?
Any one will do. One of these.
One of those. We have thus divided
the whole into sections. We have
thus divided the day into hours.
Perhaps twenty-four, the clock.
Perhaps eight, canonical. Sections
and sections. We divide prayer
into sections, the alternative
is a lump of prayer,
an entire act of living that is a prayer.
Here we return to the whole.
It is not a lump. It is very interesting.
A fullness of living as a prayer.
To divide is to make something less.
This we think about while the sun
reaches its mid-point in the sky.
It is noon, mid-day.
The heat makes me dizzy.

> "Men and women of thought and study are
> voluptuaries."
>
> "And advocate pantheism if you want to."
>
> Lyn Hejinian, *The Guard*

There are paintings that are not of this world
and there are paintings that are of this world
and which are more interesting? Of course
paintings that are of this world are more,
the spirit resides in the materials in which.
And so. Yes, so, to go from here to there
or there to here. Through through and through.
There are children for whom we are waiting
and children who are here and which are more
interesting, of course children who are here.
There are apples hanging from the tree and we can touch
      them.
I am busy making definitions when I do not know the
      boundaries.

The nation diverts monies from arms sales
to support counter-revolutionary soldiers.
Something must be done. Speak in different tongues.
Wait for nothing and anticipate anything. Desire to desire.
But if I have the gift of prophecy, and understand
all mysteries, and all knowledge, if I have all faith,
can remove mountains, and do not have charity,
I am nothing; having nothing, I possess all things.
If I can see the green streak across the sky
it is only a beginning, but a beginning
that begins in this world and continues one two three.
And some. Everything moves thoroughly moves.

Vespers / Speaking in Tongues

And vespers whispers, westering the silent moment
of imperfect noise, everything is silent and everything
has noise, we are imperfect and perfect beings,
repeating everything. The context is at stake.
That we can change. A beginning is to speak it
and speak ourselves differently in many tongues.
Tongues speak tongue twisters turn us one thoroughly
two thoroughly three after all and a child.
And four, four things: the way of an eagle
in the air, the way of a serpent on a rock,
the way of a ship in the midst of the sea,
the way of a woman with a man with a woman
with a woman with a man with a man. Something
touches each with each, she whispers, in the evening
westering. Westering a language, the way that
particular sunset vibrates in colors moving
from red to blue, nothing staying the same,
differences holding conjunctions for enduring
moments. Contradictory moments are what we endure;
we settle in in the evening, say our prayers,
prayers praise with the sound of the trumpet with
the psaltery and harp with the timbrel and dance
with stringed instruments and organs with the loud
cymbals with the high sounding cymbals with everything
that breathes and everything that does not.
And with no sound but the movement of air;
push it forward slightly with a whisper, vesper.
Truly that setting light is sweet, and comes again.

Complins Incomplete

"We eat together, that is the universal law."

"Pleasure once found, the subject knows no rest
until he can repeat it."

Roland Barthes, "An Idea of Research"
and "Reading Brillat-Savarin"

Is there a difference between reserve and reverse?
Enter everything wholeheartedly.
A sentence is that with a whole heart.
The hole art partakes of nothingness.
There never is a place to end and never was.
A cycle is that which is always repeating itself a
        bicycle is that which is always repeating itself
        twice a tricycle is that which can be musically
        represented by thirds repeating themselves.
Thunderous thirds were coming in by the hundreds.
The herd wishes to settle down for the night,
        bring water.
They have been waiting for the appearance of a child
        when there are children all about them waiting.
There never was a place to end and never is.

Side Riding

It is during the night.
Automan is a character in a one-person play.
These are the truths we hold to be self-evident.
She returns.

Move two blocks.
Prepositional qualification renders context.
Among the southern stars, find simple patterns.
The light confers.

Render possible harmonies.
She has never taken the bus to her destination.
We take the engine to be well-tuned.
This is about statement.

Counteract speech rhythms
We make probable progress in a down-draft.
If there is a path, it may have complications.
She could be talking about flying.

There is sculpture in Cincinnatti.
Doublings of consonants give a narrative broad dimension.
You may speak truthfully here.
Nature progresses.

She is speaking about silence.
Interpretations of petroglyphs deliver ambiguity.
Languages contain glottal stops.
Space is bent.

The heart breaks.
A meter maintains a thin red line.
One may be said to be *on the edge*.
What ever comes, comes.

I have written letters.
The dangerous books were contained in a labyrinth.
Friends answer friends.
Everything seemed archival.

A sculptured 'totem' appears.
Figures in the paintings looked like porno stars.
The interview posed functional questions.
Subject is always subjective.

The engine was unidentified.
Components sprawl.
Uninfringed wanderings are encouraged here.
Words maintain discoveries.

Subject statement to disclosure.
Quiet commands attentive audiences everywhere.
She could not pass by a bargain special on coffee.
She makes a revolution.

Subject it to a litmus test.
One eye is uncovered, open to investment.
Consciousness moves behind diction.
Can one be incapable of resolution?

Scratches appear on the surface.
We define everything in graphic terms.
The marvelous may be marred.
Anything may be stated.

The earth shakes.
Always, for as long as we remember, there is a penultimate.
Clouds soar on no wings.
She thinks.

Introduce a notion of relativity.
Movement depends, as we know it, on gravity.
A swimming pool across the street is not open.
Something reorganizes itself.

Make simple declarative sense.
We are in violation of these errors.
I hear the police helicopter several blocks away.
Humor makes the performer relatively less uncomfortable.

Opt for health, strive for wisdom.
The classical repeats itself inexorably.
Find the third door on the right, the one painted green.
Numbers are in place.

That terrain is rocky.
I have not ridden horses there in months.
She sequesters herself among mountains.
She writes blue monkeys.

He inscribes.
A name makes a tentative sound-object correlation.
Questions rely on punctuation for revelation.
Make the line new.

The instrument makes indentations.
A house of knowledge is a well-attended real estate development.
The film provided answers to most questions.
She comes, and slowly.

A phrase, twisted, becomes a constant.
Make mine pastrami on rye.
The two of them make quite a pair.
She'll make for the hills, and quickly.

No screens will be allowed.
Revelation means a change of climactic pattern.
Perhaps a petunia will grow here.
The earth turns.

We shall see what comes of this.
Matters only rarely get out of hand.
Stay close to the water.
Come unto me.

One reads in possible imaginings.
A tuning fork resounds in somewhat tactile vibrations.
A challenge has been issued.
Make something out of materials at hand.

There may be more here than meets the eye.
I stand uncovered before your judgement.
Lead armies astray.
Astonish the evidence.

These are moral imperatives.
He believes he has been given a mandate by the people.
Such dangers we have previously seen in divergent meanderings.
Mary goes 'round.

There are particles.
Matter rejoins itself in close quarters.
What makes a mystery comes again.
She surrounds.

It merits an adequate surrender.
Paraphrase the commands of the moment.
Say what one has to say.
Movement begins.

Increasingly, abstraction sets in.
He sets the survey sticks in the northeast quadrant.
Chew the grass softly.
Bodies emit light.

Start running toward the road.
A questionnaire prompts a mixture of serious and absurd responses.
She ably remonstrates the marchers.
Someone clasps hands and sings.

Welcome all souls.
I boil water each morning for coffee.
Take three steps forward and check your surroundings.
There is no need for alarm.

Two officers administer the trust.
Death is a sportsman on an island in a poem.
We dance and kiss in a crowded room, move to the bathroom together.
It twists blue.

Weather changes.
She hangs the clothes on the line in the late morning.
Substance abuse claims perilous lives.
Telephone rings at random intervals.

Turn in the service revenues.
Compartmentalized procedures organize the disabled.
She complains of the lack of new things.
One wants.

We receive an invitation.
Let us go to a cabin in the mountains.
These thoughts are unrelated.
Meet me in the morning.

Stand under the rain.
I remember a waterfall in a state park in Wisconsin.
We stay tuned.
Specificity applauds.

Dogs howl to the moon.
A sliver of almond makes enormous difference.
She wants to defer the reward.
Make something complete at all points.

A rainbow separates into components.
Twelve ministers received notice of policy changes.
Material witnesses were difficult to track down.
Particulate matter changes.

We try on hats for size.
Perhaps I assume too much familiarity.
A previous visitor sizes up the situation.
She warns.

The implication of perspective is the intersection of parallel lines.
She imagines an impromptu discourse on values.
Writing separates itself.
Some meanings are implied.

The aroma wafts its way upstairs.
As a child, I fell on an old plow and made a hole in my knee.
Neologisms lend identity to new enterprises.
State your business.

Visitors are encouraged.
They play a game with their hands.
Witnesses stated the facts in complete sentences.
A fly buzzed by.

A man signed a lend lease agreement.
The noise of the street made an appropriate background.
There are sometimes too many layers of experience.
Clang went the trolley.

A great distance has been traversed.
We await the arrival of appropriate personnel.
A job well done is something to enjoy.
She stands aroused.

Stamps enable passage.
I am permitted to return to an open seat.
Contractions follow one another at increasingly short intervals.
He stands revealed.

Attach two copies.
One longs for the smell of pine, life outside an office.
The confined word holds latent resonance.
He breaks his word.

He brings her blue bells.
Together we teased out the tongue of the bee to gather pollen samples.
I like to run in circles.
Stay calm, they advised.

Acrostics puzzle.
She wanted a life free of the traps made of words.
We boarded the bus dressed in red slippers.
It suffices.

I am urged.
Strong need wants to number everything nonconsecutively.
She moves with halting rhythms.
Song emerges.

The lines, unless otherwise noted, are regular.
This means not a whit.
Strands of light are allowed through the window.
Dust settles.

He begins reading a writing.
The truth of it will come out in the wash.
Two orioles sing on a live wire.
Cars crash.

Among friends, a vow matters.
We write for necessity, from syllables.
Fire stirs his imagination.
Fright makes the matter.

Chocolate tastes self-righteous.
He makes from mint a twisted meaning.
Explanation implies order.
Hierarchies topple.

She stands on retrieved ground.
Implicit in the ordering is a sense of stated surprise.
Movement is terrain traversed in time.
Perhaps something develops.

Frustrate supposed directedness.
State multiple realities in sequential orders.
One demonstrates manners of moving triangles.
Procedures are instated.

There are hints of movement.
States topple when their codes are opened to inspection.
Take large doses of political vision.
Something tumbles down.

She assumes difficulties.
Stay with your initial impulse, carry it through stages of work.
A string of mountain ranges punctuates the landscape.
Geology disrupts.

It closes itself off at the ends.
Endless numeration indicates potential astronomy.
If there is no way out, go in.
She allows him to wander freely.

Love allows the language to play.
Perhaps permission will be granted.
An unnamed monitor lets the day out.
Requests are granted.

Stay by the door.
Breezes contend with flags for information.
Populaces take command of endowed powers.
Stranger things have happened.

May fairs celebrate the blossoming.
Inquire as to the nature of scents.
Within a certain range, the spread of pollen follows regular patterns.
All else is accidental.

She surrounds syntax.
There is no such thing as a lack of connection.
All symptoms are assumed to be related.
The market jumps.

Finesse is not required.
Somewhat reluctantly, she hesitates in mid-air.
Everything hangs together in duly noted lines.
Guitars strum.

Nine marks on the page signify.
Relationships are either exposed or found lacking.
Contradiction interests me.
The rates vary.

Fire demands attention.
He attempts to live as variously as is possible.
The members have sampled the responses.
She donates tenderness.

Political parties make mistakes.
People are gathered to show their anger graciously.
The lack of control raised questions in their minds.
Walk up the steepest trail.

She completes the act.
The state takes action in roundabout ways.
He notices random activity in the subatomic realm.
No one asks questions.

Predominantly, we wonder.
First time there, they thought they were in heaven.
If he dies of love, he'll be the first.
They measure their responses.

Straw hats are the order of the day.
She gathers scattered feathers in the desert.
Sacred rites maintain oppressive orders.
Stir fry fortifies.

Connect the dots from religion to government.
Of the people sweetly sounds, a warning cry perhaps.
Functional illiteracy becomes a stated then ignored problem.
Homeless people walk vacant streets.

Halfway, the children begin to sing.
The rallying cry makes the throat hoarse.
Of necessity, they take a cause to the street, and find reasons.
She has begun.

Accidents happen.
Progressions of events make lists obsolete in a hurry.
Three traffic accidents have involved friends during the last two weeks.
Maintain the peace.

Once she started, she found cessation difficult.
Biology is a determining factor.
Children do not issue forth with ease.
Men do not always understand, or rarely.

Come quickly, and stay in place.
Frightened monitors tracked the light's movement across the sky.
Mythology never predicted such enormous changes.
Keep the pace.

Across the table, she strives for improvement.
He meant it when he said he mistrusted the state spokesman.
Trust led the way to enabling compromise.
The reigns tighten.

She sits huddled over.
I am asked to write a book of hours.
There has never been a war that was not primarily about money.
She irons clothes for a journey.

Large stones of agate fill the road.
Winds gather force to the top of the canyon.
Forces struggle to end their dominance.
She tends the fire while I read stories aloud.

A dog howls in the near distance.
Two handles in tandem free the water supply.
We should walk up the road.
Content becomes less abstruse.

Defy semantic expectations.
Single statements complete the work at each juncture.
She holds palette and brushes and looks intently.
Fire clears the area.

Artists misunderstand the public.
Such statements, misconstrued, lead to erratic behavior.
Freedom rings a bell, walks the next mile, turns.
She wishes.

From that moment, they believed.
The pollination process peaked when we visited the mountain.
She identifies each bird in its natural habitat.
We construe.

There is no purely personal history.
The social register abides by certain notions of embedded privacy.
French cut swimwear has been popular for a few years.
Stress multiplies.

Inquire into the nature of completion.
Dilapidated buildings lend older neighborhoods an air of possibility.
Councils move at the pace of contractors paid by the hour.
Sirens call.

Answer them.
Parallel lines intersect by means of their resonance.
Cats rarely forget people who have been kind to them.
Planes cast shadows.

Signals mingle.
Perhaps something is explained by the fact of my father having taught
        geometry.
They did not know if responses could be said to be adequate.
Friends correlate.

Thousands of autos park.
The topographical map was tacked onto the bathroom wall.
Members check their locations with one another.
Time passes.

He remarked on the probabilities.
They passed time with conversation concerning the political assassinations.
Noone remained convinced of the improprieties.
Ideas should lead to action.

Everything seems to be for sale.
The government protected a large stand of virgin white pine.
They granted asylum to more than one political tyrant.
Lapses of attention are expected.

Focus the senses.
Gather information previous to revolution.
They looked at each other across the aisle with great surprise.
An explosion was totally unexpected.

Cooks stir soups.
Cold storage seemed to be in order.
I remembered the madrona trees.
Sympathy walks.

Forty miles away the cabin sits empty, we remember.
Perhaps events recur.
Individual action does not guarantee consciousness.
In the next room, she irons.

Try not to worry.
She gives him instructions constantly.
Listen anyway, wandering attentions are dangerous.
Leaves fall.

Light bounces.
Her eyes still attract me.
If there is no knowledge without reflection, language enters.
She senses my gaze.

She gave a doll a ceramic head.
Notations become necessity, act on them.
Time expands to fill one's consciousness.
She acted accordingly.

He heard bells in the distance.
Several people bring presents for the child.
Civilians surrender their means of self-government.
Consider the effects.

They lay together beside the opening.
Side by side sentences stand, and groups of sentences.
Reward meets the nourished.
Consent abolishes passivity.

Memory is an aid to memory.
The neighbors burn leaves in a contained space.
I planted peach trees as a teenager.
Attentive eyes take in nothing that is not of interest.

Women are underrepresented.
Two feet provide a basis for understanding.
Do not comply with inconsiderate organizers.
Take nothing for granted.

The state trammels the rights of the unpriveleged.
Forget justice, attend to the demands of survival.
Sometimes we leave for the hills, the still natural world.
Words suffice.

She takes a southern route.
Fatherhood stands in the scene of a probable future.
Tell me a tale of bravery.
The western sky brightens.

The mechanic conveys a plan.
What more, one wonders, can armies do.
In the fields lies the moral conscience of a people.
She puts it into action.

Stress filters itself.
The automobile yearns for lubricatory satisfaction.
Hindsight produces errors of oversight.
Stay with what you do well.

Never move, he advised me.
It has not been included in my training.
The ground underfoot was boggy, requiring a footsure step.
Make lively.

Bitter weather accompanies emotional upheaval.
Change aspects of the personality which are unfortunate.
The dentist strikes the molar with surgical precision.
Armies ready.

Full studies of optics move beyond perspective.
With eyes nearly closed, she sees color in terms of black and white.
All visual information achieves equal status.
See things clearly, and see them whole.

We eliminate the need for protection.
Power struggles win nothing.
Change the face of the building.
They remove themselves.

Final decisions may be delayed.
One applies for a range of opportunities.
Secretaries collate copies of readiness orders.
Relief is in sight.

Water pardons the skin.
Hard work proves a base for consolation.
Sentences march by in acausal procession.
She sings wildly.

Melodies form vibrations into more or less regular patterns.
Performers enter the hall without regimentation.
Military discipline constricts imaginative action.
She pauses.

Another artist wants to sell me a printing press.
We are waiting for a check.
I must pay back rent and loan a sculptor rent money.
This is the way an art community works.

A man wants to buy a printing press and keep it in my studio.
Pray at regular intervals.
Hours divide days.
Books distribute prayers.

Call tomorrow and see.
Let us inspect the merchandise.
A certain bravado won the day.
I am moved.

The first person constructs itself.
The person constructs other entities, including sentences.
A book moves from idea to artifact to commodity.
She asks me to write a book of hours.

Examine the meaning of prayer.
Make notations at certain times of day.
A writer's imperatives are commands tried out on oneself.
She understands my hair.

A glass of wine fortifies the spirit.
Consumption of alcohol may be related to breast cancer in women.
Nothing remains sacred once published.
This has not always been the function of books.

The written word once moved from private to public use.
Writing is a reminder of what words we tell ourselves.
They couldn't decide to sell the house.
Tell me a riddle.

Among morphemes he looks for commonality.
Equal time demands equal work.
I have never before written in aphorisms.
Stand the strain.

Fruit affects the shape on one's face.
Individuals find no final answers here.
Trips to Texas are rewarded with children.
He sings to their child.

Change the face of your lives.
The toilet flushes with admirable ease.
Pure products of multinational corporations go crazy.
We eat somewhat less.

Do not leave the primary corridor.
Something grows organically, disregarding linearity.
Steady progression can be summarily denied.
She rejects closure.

Symphonies stir the air.
This is literal, vibrations move.
She wants to be with me tonight listening, hungry.
Call later.

Freezing temperatures are not expected.
We looked down, through the canyon, at the stretching city lights.
The extent of the mountain dwarfs its inhabitants.
Cities cease.

We have evidence of human habitation.
Cities build roads across archaeology.
Pragmatism directs all vision toward future rewards.
Act now, save later.

Marginality befits his poems.
We sought the horses in the far corners of the field.
Someone strays here often, dropping hints.
Lovers search.

Hours parallel horrors.
Seek and you shall find appropriate words.
Technology speeds up some things, slows down others.
Forget nothing.

He committed a hatchet-job.
Muddleheadedness carries no known reward.
Responsibility requires one to accept it unflinchingly.
Turn around.

The cat sits on the ledge outside the window.
Sometimes she moves with considered steps.
He has enjoyed baking bread in the past.
Domesticity is suspect.

Water bursts its confines.
The book becomes something other than container.
Small wood pieces functioned as dividers in the box.
He longs to make something discontinuous.

A man forgets his past.
The poem functions as an instrument of thought.
They pause a moment by the roadside to catch their wits.
An air of difference reigned.

Monarchy vanishes.
I wait for a man concerned about a book.
Birds fly between land and vessel.
Blue satisfies.

They listen for dissonance.
Sentence production conveys possibility.
Always there will be a future, its content is unknown.
She ventures into prediction.

Venture capital signifies desire.
Angels populate the verso of its pages.
He remains capable of continuous thought, in time.
All desire is the desire for meaning.

Pants stretch to fit.
I am fasting for a day.
Vitamins taken without prior food float through the body.
Systems need cleaning.

Political needs can never be satisfied.
He sees the public sphere as a place requiring secrecy.
Missiles had not previously been mentioned.
The stars have no knowledge of war.

They tithe regularly.
She wonders if auras are a reflection or an emission of light.
The life of the spirit survives in arid lands.
Let it commence.

They capitalize on the situation.
To name a product is not to own it.
The struggle for sovereignty becomes all-consuming.
She capitulates.

Images move.
Still pictures in revolution require an act of juxtaposition.
The food on the table appeals to a variety of senses.
Scattered noise disappoints.

Confidence matters.
She travels to a distant city on a river, stays in a hotel.
History gathers discrete events and graphs them in time.
Patterns repeat in variation.

The sky darkens.
Weeks pass and we hope for rain.
His graciousness was not gleaned from previous encounters.
We walk across the riverbed.

Plastic animals constitute imaginary zoos.
He was kept in a confined place for too long.
Acts of faith leap among semantic gaps.
She turns her head.

A small child, girl, laughs and falls asleep.
The man sitting next to me at the symphony falls asleep and snores.
The woman to my right wears a white sweater and disappears.
Intermission interrupts.

Publicity consumes.
Finally, the check is not in the mail.
Render unto him what rightfully belongs.
She frowns.

I speak across miles and states.
She arrives, is driven over green hilly land, crosses a river.
Hot days make driving an uneasy prospect.
The women confer.

Stars burn.
Outside, she lay in the sun until her skin blushed.
The cats did not come in before night fell.
The table is set.

Domestic and public subjects interact.
Such lives we lead, every day.
Political motives are at the base of all action.
Some words have become suspect.

He fasted for a day, taking only liquids.
Night fell with random illumination.
One wants to walk with no destination.
They forgot themselves.

The vegetables were pierced with skewers.
Clouds promised rain and appeared in the west.
Some possibilities recur with great frequency.
But it did not rain.

Time advances.
She chooses to spend much time in the mountains.
He reads much, takes walks on Tuesdays.
Perhaps they will live by the sea.

Train a dog to do new tricks.
On the witness stand, the military men revealed all.
From above, a loud and long laughter was heard.
Presidents know.

Products sell.
She longed for a place in the country.
He had difficulty deciding about the future.
Limits are what we live inside.

It grows inordinately.
The cat refuses to go out the door when opened.
He attempts to write a few sentences about music.
The theme interrupts.

Strange how things develop.
For now, let us take brief walks under stars.
Repeat the dominant chord until a signal is given.
She attempts to gain their respect.

She stole the song.
The violins entered together in time, notes of dissonance.
Everything has been underwritten by the company.
They increase the tempo.

Failed marriages have been investigated.
The comet appeared as a mere brush of the sky.
What light considers may be admired.
Taste it first.

Quick movements are preferred.
They played on the porch with three children and three dogs.
She plays the cello as if she was born to it.
There are no natural military men.

Sinews tighten.
He doubts his abilities, but only temporarily.
The music that lasts can not be ignored.
Straighten the room.

Days become hotter.
Eat nothing one day, plenty the next.
He runs laps around real and imaginary ovals.
She prepares the report.

He bakes bread.
Seldom is there time to be alone.
They need each other, a complementary effect.
Salads are tossed.

She turns things upside down.
In the woods there are no dull moments.
A dog howls at the moon in the distance.
He wants to go on a hike.

Fits are common among apes.
I dropped him off at the mall to buy pants.
The first thought may have been the most complete.
The parts fit together.

She wore a tuxedo.
Expectations are denied, then reversed.
Explore the nature of sentence relations.
Readers act and react.

Words act, they form relationships.
Ultimatums are never easy to swallow.
The road in front of our house is short and curvy.
Across the street they play ball.

Summer is coming in.
Somewhere, not here, a cuckoo sings.
The clock gains five minutes each day.
I remember taking off my clothes in a prairie.

Intentions are discovered as one continues.
He forgets the first words.
The wood withstands years of weathering.
For the night, friends visit.

She thinks of the midwest as a green place.
In a painting, the edge of the sky is green.
They celebrate the rejuvenation of the swimming pool.
All else succeeds.

The reader spoke of a mechanic who had died.
A clown he was, and perhaps it was a joke.
Monologues may be poems or anything.
She interrupts rudely and unnecessarily.

Someone reads a story about UFO visitations.
He speaks in many voices.
I could and would not remain for the next poet.
Some things are lost.

A black sweater and a green scarf have disappeared.
Change the channel and see what is worth watching.
Many poems are not as well made as television programs.
Images veer to the left.

Disagreements do not always produce dialectical mechanisms.
They are mistaken if they think of poetry as glamorous.
Personalities are not what we want to talk about.
Excuse me while I kiss the sky.

The tape has finished playing.
Her taste ranges from rococo to art deco.
A certain bitterness creeps into the tone, lose it.
The quartet inspires.

Most of the best art begins and ends with a question.
She felt her performance was the best in that role.
Again I want to wander secluded trails.
Everything washes away.

Fields lie fallow.
He conducted the orchestra for the last time.
It is a sin to pay for nuclear weapons.
Candidates resign.

She directed the participants.
The cactus has been blossoming for several days.
She mixed colors with precision to find a welcoming blue.
Perceptions change.

They read together.
Too many artists meekly accept marginality.
The workers were getting nowhere, seeking escape.
Skies open.

She strides forward.
They have come to share their fortunes.
The same individuals receive the same awards.
Few are chosen.

Four sides proclaim a geometric figure.
In championing discursive poetry the right claims populism as its own.
Listen carefully to the words and what stands behind them.
Men are outspoken.

Claims against his righteousness have been made.
He struts a warped personality as though it is to be cherished.
Defensiveness will not get you anywhere.
Champion found causes.

Redemption sets in.
Walks across frozen lakes alter the stepping ground.
She exercises for pleasure, consuming many liquids.
Love steps lively.

Dinners are served.
Someone I love sits more than thirty thousand feet high.
We imagine ourselves in different locations.
The skin tautens.

String along.
A bear has been seen in the woods before.
When the trail ends, move toward water.
It loses its edge.

Salt, flour, and yeast combine for hearty flavor.
I offer you a crust of bread.
Make mine light and refreshing.
She smiles, knowingly.

She sheds her clothes.
Make something in which sincerity is not a question.
Collaborate on breathtaking projects, breathe deeply together.
We crawled inside.

Caverns are both foreboding and comfortable.
Magic wands became a scarce commodity.
Production methods sag behind the imagination.
She turns toward the window.

I bake bread, the smell surrounds us.
She delights the imagination with lithe movement.
Make one thousand sentences which say something.
Everything relates.

Every human being on the planet entered through a woman.
We memorize our historical origins.
Russian officials quote Lenin often to legitimize their actions.
Americans eulogize but rarely use the founding fathers.

Intellect beguiles.
She arouses my higher passions.
Return tonight, and bring your body with you.
Eat hearty.

A man learns sixty-four languages.
In using language, communication always figures.
They never intended to tell stories other than the truth.
Stop shuffling your feet, the teacher said.

A language is like a maze.
Step into the room and measure your surroundings.
They interpret imperatives as possible instructions.
Continue drawing a straight line.

Functions recall earlier embarassments.
A minimum wage is not a livable wage.
A candidate is an adulterer, the president is a murderer.
He helps build hydroelectric plants in Nicaragua.

She drives too fast for me.
Good advice is not the same as good instructions.
Direct the army into the ocean.
He washes his hands.

They question the world.
Someone graphs the incidences of AIDS.
Young women are believed to be at risk.
Stay close to home.

She is unsure of herself.
Color slides document years of creative work.
Each piece sums up everything she knows.
She uses the right tool for the job.

He stands under a large rock.
Hummingbirds require many flowers to support their lives.
The mating aerial dance began weeks ago.
She finds solace in the natural world.

Wander along the river.
She walks with head bent down and finds incredible rocks.
Together they ladder down the bluff to the beach.
Seeing is more complicated than believing.

People of long travels camped here.
Dancers on the reservation joke about being photographed.
The beads made all colors possible.
He states things in odd ways.

We all go to junk yards sometime.
My father kept his hair short, a military style.
The right combination has never been found.
Just whistle.

We send letters and talk on the phone.
Editors call dismissive pats on backs "encouragement."
You have a new son I long to see and know.
Dismiss unerringly trivial correspondence.

Communities are built.
Trust those who support your efforts despite their questions.
We go to events because we think they are important.
Respect a variety of opinions.

Offer no blind endorsements.
There are several establishments, rendering accomplishment into stone.
The tablets are incised with computer designs.
Dialogues ensue.

A house of knowledge opens its doors.
The branches of the pine tree are the points of new life.
The puppies sought and found milk from a recent mother not their own.
Take the trouble.

She teaches drawing.
Married, she wonders what it is like to be married.
I try to keep her from being too exhausted.
The nights pass.

They keep cool.
The year moves toward an Arizona summer.
What began as a simple project became something else.
The cat sleeps.

He saved us fifty dollars.
The sculptor becomes funnier the more difficult the task becomes.
He attempted to make social change through the art community.
Few listened.

Over the long haul, she struggles to keep herself active.
Tomorrow a new movie arrives at the video store.
We need to eat more fruit.
Change your heart.

I read a prose poem titled *Arizona* and understand it.
In creating a literary work, there is an analogy to perspective.
She disturbed the deepest of images to see what might ensue.
Soup thickens.

To my surprise, the window washer worked.
Suddenly what was murky becomes clear.
It becomes necessary to title a work.
They saw a wide world.

She put a number of things side by side.
She wanted to make her sculpture more solid.
Items too light or insubstantial fly away or disappear.
She looks up.

He stands aside.
I am interrupted by a telephone call.
Sentences accumulate one by four.
Move ahead.

He skips a day.
Some days they run around an oval track.
Misbegotten wealth weighs heavily.
She returns to a different place.

Stripes are preferred.
Sounds are heard in uneven sequence.
The job of the poet is to compose.
We refer to the study.

The nature of art is enigmatic.
Public behavior allows immorality to pass as patriotism.
We scrutinize the candidates in their bedrooms.
Journalism instructs.

The issues are ignored.
A president arranges assistance for terrorists and murderers.
The eyes of a nation stay tuned to television sets.
Witness are subpoenaed.

We think of a life by water.
In the meantime, termites are noticed.
Stranger events beseech her extraordinary talents.
Congregations sing hymns.

Forensics exercise a few muscles.
The differences amounted to cosmetic surgery.
Political turmoil puts armies to sleep, we can hope.
We can hope.

String bikinis are not seen here.
Fashionable men secretly profit from inside stock market information.
The newspaper article mentions crack in Harlem.
Discount the obvious.

She frees the flag.
Real drug problems occur in the financial district.
The world of commerce believes in the morality of profit.
Fly away.

He suspects the president.
A vain man sends oversize armies to small islands.
The actions of white South Africans are products of bigoted fear.
No one is free of prejudice.

The pigs call loudly.
She asks survey questions on the telephone.
It seems that everyone wants to define you.
These sentences carry no definitions.

Suspend judgement.
He spends his income on necessities.
We believe in conducting our own wars of judgement.
She replies.

Among groups of statements, several cohere.
She squandered delight among several bottles.
Recent studies show relationships between unacknowledged legislators.
He has made such observations before.

Encounter probable futures.
Quick physical movements elicit the cat's response.
Reaction delays have been shown to be negligible.
We go considerable distance to state the obvious.

He seeks approval.
Someone suffers in an enclosed space from the heat.
He almost trembles with excitement as she removes her clothes.
He takes the clock from the dresser.

Substantial change has occured.
She knows how to recognize glacial drifts.
We slept together on the beach and looked forward to sunrise.
Repetitions occur unerringly.

She longs to cross the westward ocean.
I have solidly embraced the local geography.
Regarding each other, they allowed themselves new vulnerability.
Fill the gaps.

She summons him.
The assumptions were strictly heterosexual.
They have considered another politics altogether.
Sentences generate.

The last movement begins.
A ruled page constructs a reality.
Flush left, the cry returned from the outback.
He moves veritable octopi.

She considers her position.
He does not like the alternative.
Commitment is important to at least one of them.
She wants to peer ahead.

Fortresses protect those outside.
Feudal relations are replaced by pretended democracies.
Equal opportunity is only a sound.
Each tone receives equal duration.

Strong lines control the gene pool.
He believes Americans are becoming less intelligent.
The election of actors produced a political sublife.
Render the obvious unintelligible.

I do not speak the language of carpenters.
He made the machine work with insufficient tools.
The winds have been blowing from the east.
Climatic patterns change.

She thinks the end is anticlimactic.
For once the answers were not hidden.
They questioned whether the water supply was adequate.
In a pinch, militaries master.

She continually thrusts.
Pelvic relationships may be thrilling but shallow.
We wanted to prove a point to the observers.
Some things merit second chances.

The ensemble specializes in chamber music.
He is equally interested in eras of change.
The conservative approach merits its fate.
An ill wind whispers.

The light was minimal but well directed.
He questioned the possibility of continuing.
On a cloudy night, he regained his composure.
She strayed toward insecurity.

The telephone waits.
The envelopes are ready to be mailed.
Everything stands behind the smaller cat.
Pears do not last.

Choose the appropriate text.
Her art accomodates objects she finds in cities and out.
Their attitude of initial skepticism led to final lapses of commitment.
They mistake everything in their search for objectivity.

The central character is always changing.
Objects are thrown in the way, they make the path variable.
Try and walk directly from one place to another.
Reality is curved.

The baseball pitcher was famous for his fast ball.
Nothing meanders straight ahead.
He became an advertising ploy.
Digits lie.

Irascibility is welcomed.
Traitors confuse the colors of the uniforms.
Armies disperse themselves after prolonged conflicts.
They desired an imminent collapse.

She reads poems on the train platform.
The preference for a single strategy is avoided.
Conflict has been eschewed in favor of complexity.
Make the reader a participant.

Something solves.
He was unaware of the presence of a problem.
She walked around the interferences.
Make yourself known.

They raised their voices.
I listen to the string quartet on the tape player.
The question of voice is irrelevant to the poem.
Self destructs.

Continuity implies will in time.
She will mark the end of the line.
Punctuation clearly formed the argument.
He enlists my help.

Former nuns celebrate new women.
Renouncements have been accepted graciously.
They flee from me, who once sought my favor.
Consider the case.

I wear a watch.
We place each sentence in a paragraph, giving context.
Text places itself against text.
The words form a kind of army.

A friend seeks coherence in his work.
She gave me a reason to celebrate belief.
Someone gives a speech to inanimate objects.
We hesitate to desire.

Never stop the wanting.
She collapsed on top of me after exaltation.
Among high places she collects unusual stones.
I stop somewhere forever.

Final apologies meet with refusals.
The accusations of criminal activity are categorically denied.
A president believes he can do no wrong.
Many listen and question.

We want to vote for a woman.
Higher office does not require senses of responsibility.
Her sensual responses are multiple.
We maintain an alert.

Each utterance can be heard as a song.
The way to understand is through meditation.
She sees a text as a place to play.
We really did wander in the woods.

Inside Moves,

Punctual Matters

Salve salvage in the spin.
Endorse the splendor splashes;
stylize the flawed utility;
prop a malign or failing light —
but know the whirlwind is our commonwealth.

> Gwendolyn Brooks,
> "The Second Sermon on the Warpland"

Attraction sits on a pinhead.

Love rests on finer points.

We locate near fault lines

       or hair-pin curves.

Rest easy. Everything snaps into place.

Attend to sense of mending.

Missile silos revise architects' paradigms.

Refrain from smoking, please,

      children have been abandoned.

Spend wisely. Hours slip away.

Anatomically, choose an erotics of search.

Neighborhoods criticize traffic plans.

Her movement toward him confirmed

    a new definition of articulate.

Hold on. I'm coming.

Across the street, a school waited for students.

She changed her mind in the midst of a blue jacket.

Address voluptuous matters,

      signs of educated hunger.

Forget nothing. The tide is in.

Adjust the loom, begin the weaving.

Cast forth nets of words,

See what catches, what craves,

      what waters move above ground.

Wait, restless. Time is a made thing.

Compare a social bond to text.

Sing enraptured, church hearts drawn taut.

I remember Sunday mornings before service,

    closed in choir-robe closets.

Do not threaten rupture. Seals break.

Crayola rules a fractured commerce.

Stun a world with traced magenta.

Imagine, she thought, this sex dream

      dispersed in a morning's coffee.

New skin tightens. Fear inherits thinking.

Cartoons deliver political blows.

Steering mechanisms give way to free fall,

We bump over curves into spare deserts,

    parts scattered to all corners.

Remember the underground, not lost.

Crescendos are learned.

In a yard of weeds, lend water.

Dry goods beckon signs of change,

       market economies refer to nothing.

Manipulate the stock. Love disorders.

What does a person invest here?

A voice, perhaps, and where.

Turn that talent to use,

      words lead to language.

Counter every move. We provide.

Televised masquerades, salesmanship as communication.

What does *one* invest in *mass*?

Turn twice around,

      dial a code.

The counters mount horses of oppression.

Thought control hides as recreation.

These solutions are easy.

In a time when nothing settles,

      everything vibrates openly.

Stand aside. The games begin.

Specific applications are open.

This for that, metaphor tingles.

Skin opens to fleshy pulp,

      inside leads to outside.

For a time, some *other* waits.

A play of surface is thin disguise.

Meaning attracts and falls short of seduction.

The story, begin again,

      tell it like a dream.

Touch matters. We mingle freely.

Everything stands up to be counted.

What leaves raked in yard?

Spaces between, the numbers arrive,

      or some motion is missing.

The parts cohere. Edges leave nothing to choice.

The language repairman has arrived,

Requires a field of operation.

Her fees paid,

      no dollar value assumed.

Free the verbs. We name to name.

Triads of trumps disappear in sand.

Saturation points to erotic delight.

Desire to desire,

      this daylight warms cardinal points.

Full fathom, lie quiet.

Brew the broth fitful, discover water.

From pie to plaster, domesticate yourself.

She comprehends dreams,

      drops hints of escape.

One wants sex, wakes up knowing.

Surprise, what we say returns.

Wandering line speaks loud life,

Puts one foot before another,

one at a time.

Not random, upon my honor.

Movement becomes a struggle against lines.

Or within, what moves within

Or not, everything moves

      thorough, bits at a time.

Perhaps random. References decide.

Postcards arrive daily at any location.

You speak to me beyond sleep.

For method,

      refer to angry cookbooks.

Culture disposes itself toward dismembering.

Put in something sexual, tonight can't utter.

Framed windows seal nothing out.

Up and down, that out

      or in, you want me now.

Take nothing. Nations rise.

Pincushions put a stop to points.

Sharpen scissors, bake bread, cut stalks.

Self to social resonance,

there is no road unmarked.

Feed someone. Begin with sustain.

Does anything develop farther than eye scans?

Set sparks, chora wants no chaos.

Untumbled, sit around a fire,

        sing to no one hearing,

Light something. Shed new tears.

Imperatives kill kind requests deserving.

Serve, I serve, what purpose,

To know a thing in silence,

       nothing is silent.

Compose a line. Garden rows meander.

Flirtation causes solitary abrasions.

The milk does not curdle in winter.

Cabin fever occurs so seldom,

> we make love above the ice.

Fire warns. Warm heaven rises.

Political lines are drawn and quartered.

The raw smell of fish attends a social.

For a reason,

    I ask you to stay with me.

Stir often. Wake up when batter thickens.

For education, stun the universe.

Who wants to know, shell or pumpkin?

Take decisions lightly,

      stay away from the water.

This much we know. He stays to arrive.

A mustard poultice makes medical history.

For the record, erase the woeful strain.

Candidates stump the nation,

      bumper stickers err gramatically.

Stop. This line makes a turn.

Make a wish that moves as music.

Saxophone causes skin to open.

Take you, for example,

 surround me with stretched limbs.

Do it again. It never composes.

When to confront what worrisome echoes.

Shift to leeward, that winding fawn.

Drink from a silver-edged pond at morning,

linger there, fall in.

Don't let it. Snap the streak.

I wait somewhere, stopping for air.

Curse a purity of diction, alter vision.

When it appears clearly,

    look again.

Keep eyes open. It all changes.

Any thing forms an insatiable mouth.

Of eating we seek certain knowledge.

Mine, for example,

      to gain entrance.

Two stable fortresses wake. Feign sleep.

Four separate picture planes, close together,

Make a cross appear in space.

This teaches terror,

   our parts.

Buy time. Tell tales.

Accuse a lover of neglecting one leg.

Stain a pillow, not with sleep.

Recount a new dream,

   keep some part a mystery.

Aprons fly. Cook a fine breakfast.

Another day in the life of a word

Makes a difference in universal grammars.

Tree structures abstain,

       this is imagined hardship.

Fork over. One loves a spoon.

Ask me anything, but expect response

Rather than answer. Frayed coat-tails

Mean a father's garment,

       across the ocean years ago.

Keep your shirt on. Politeness lasts.

Step on a stone and break a vessel.

Break three and have an apology ready.

She narrates her travels,

       temples stand on walls.

Slide the light. It could be another.

You decide at the beginning when to end.

The behavior leaves nothing open or not.

Islands can't be,

      unless eyes close.

Dance with me. Let nothing bear witness.

Someone we met presents plays,

Produces flamenco, travels in Spanish widely.

Can anyone read

      and buy books to live?

Move aisles. Speak in asides.

Five framed possibles occur at random.

Everything metaphors, nothing smiles openly.

Language enters a plane,

      geometry is what my father taught.

Remember the present. Steep angles of light.

Nothing can be said politically or tremors.

The social drama forgets no tyrant.

Falling religion presents ultimatums,

     makes choices into requirements.

Centers hold. Feet shuffle away.

The power of horror confirms a hypothesis.

That language poeticizes revolution stands firm.

All desire is desire

for meaning or desire.

Short sessions shock. Fear is real.

One envies what one has not,

Erase what nothing can know.

Above all meaning,

　　　some syllable sucks air.

Forge steel. Hard metal sends machines flying.

For knowledge a woman sacrifices something else.

Take advantage of the last light.

Dance without me,

      that sense of sex can wait.

Come back. It holds up, take it in.

Fritter away time, but not yourself.

These lines say nothing about buying.

It aches a little,

      this learned urge to spend.

Concentrate. Nothing leaves you.

He said, with as little purchase on the soul as possible.

What merits soul, when nothing sounds?

Surface can't suffice,

   lean to one side.

Flee. Return soon.

It can't happen this way.

Enter, reader, take a chair, measure self.

Upon a floor in some room,

      attend to intricate markings.

Make sure. Rest uncomfortably with flatness.

These lines say little of dieing, but see.

Every mark ends, serif or not.

Words introduce words,

she flies into place.

Straddle fences. What does it feel like?

What resolves? Can you touch me

With a tenuous or raw fleshiness?

Don't stop moving,

or nothing comes to fruition.

Can anything live? Stop.

Hopeful Buildings

A sky hangs over the earth, another inflates the room.

Stormy weather unites tribal factions

Where nothing succeeds like oppress.

Blocks bear letters, become site for architects' wordings,

Chosen models by chosen leaders bear chosen delights.

Selection involves subtraction, multiples divide.

A fifth of beauty becomes drink for millions;

No manna here provides dividends.

No money here defines evidence

Starvation litters streets where once rodeo paraded.

A horse is a horse of course of course unless

Of course the house is dead, no steersman provided.

We learn elementary functions and can not,

Excepting dials are turned to proper channels,

Convince the powers that be not to be.

Frightened children encourage vivid portrayals, what helps?

Fighting kindred have courage, live in portals, not yelps.

Unseen kitchens give eggs and vegetables, tables turn

Themselves, with some help from calendars, what day is it?

Bicycles gain motors, fly without wings —

One dreams on the street where she lives.

In a family, she wears pants and father comes home

Or not, the pictures on the wall have come down

And none is the worse for wear, not this year.

End one issue terse or fair, know this mirror

Unites a sense of self to world, not spoken in code

Or surrendered to a father, child waits for words

No one teaches, woman or some other kind of friend

Who reaches into a night and pulls out constellation,

Reconstitutes a dream with interchangeable parts —

No person accepts a role that won't change to lead or follow.

We move somewhere here, look out the window, gauge the light.

Free toothsome air, hear a shout of wind, oh change the night.
Not every syllable contributes to plot, syntax baffles.
Everything can be removed and still a site stands
Not denuded, not bombed. Restructuring follows,
And is never finished, *Or* has not yet begun to fight,
Some enemies are known, their names signify signs,
Friends hum in the wings of sound, angels survive avalanche —
Shuffle the blocks and buildings; make a new sentence.

Slow flow the clocks and stillness shakes a nuisance tense.
Stand aside, she said, I'm scared of change but see the need.
So do we all, or live in a dry river bed, wait for flood.
Monthly waters are models to live by, or make children
Wait for food, the end of the line changes the sense.
We know that and little else, how to bake a loaf perhaps
Or bite the bullet that feeds us, may the force mix
Strands with baked good, ounces of tablespoons answer.

Star switch ached moods, chances of able tunes after.
Swear you won't tell me I'm mad, I'll read you lines.
Lines of age, lines of change, post office lines indicate
A willingness to communicate, though alphabets in disarray
Provide opportunities to amass monies as well as good will.
Return to the city, the blocks still stand, facades have changed to color.
And what is wrong with that? Question me an answer —
Fiddle with everything and listen to music.

Handle with airy ring, endless amusement.
Shadows tell us not as much as mirrors divided
Into surface sense and sight's reflected glory.
Take time to hear a story, listen for openings —
Strategy aligns itself with witness, creates a mess,
Approaches message, entry requires a door
But designers have options therein, make choices.
Not shy changes for mirth, a brother creates a loom.

An Eye for the Distance

At Text

You can only move around, what you are trying to say, to believe in trouble. To curve reality and time, organize in the trajectory of the species. Our mind is extravagant. A reading back, a beginning back reading forward, a necessity envisioning a child. What moves forward, young and isolated. But child is a state we haven't entered, minus the lines. Line everything up against the wall, a walled city, when you walked on the street last night and wanted a popsicle, and we bought them, and ate them, one lime, one tamarindo. To not know what tamarindo is. I've a mind to, the poem can be like a walk, can be, like a life. And why would one want to, the diminishment of experience. To turn the astonishment of the encounter into a monotonic descriptive poem. There are other places, and shadows. A shadow is easy to make, it disappears sometimes. If there is not a subject there is not a subject, the way you entwine my body, I yours, hair rising between thighs, a salt taste of biscuits. And now we read back, and there. and there. A walk in a grove in a place I have only seen at night when you have no shadow.

Next a reading mine

a reading. and what is it. this moves which way. upon the face of a coin. a language may have not been considered as a tissue, and why not? the ephemera of an object, upon a rock. there is no such thing as a no. where? could it have happened in someone's conception of an unconscious? perhaps the wine perhaps the wanting. a certain impulse toward the lyrical was seen to be a line disguising itself as heterogeneity. a chorus perhaps but not harmonic. no such thing as an empty spot in the field. if there are children waiting have they seen the weapons of their fathers? a lawn mower imposes an order and process too can be the site of an oppression. a certain I remembers a father there, maintaining a certain method of mowing as correct. not understood why. permissions are taken away. the comfort of using such tools as a level has never been mine. there are exceptions. uncomfortable hegemonies with the assured and complicit agreements of a mother. how does one deviate? to hone in on a number, mathematics betray the mathematician. we have seen uncertain examples. I remember learning to ride a bicycle, a line was anything but straight. if a child is left in a tree from which she can not or perhaps he, that is, descend, will the consequences be enormous? they have not been known not to be. in an autumn moving through fallen leaves in one city or another, among two livings. a sense of the presence of water is enormous. a hum of autobiograph under the periods. make this mine or hum a fine madness. dramatic interplay, yes, the metaphor is missing. an eye for the distance.

Remains

Approach from the edge. A magnet closes a door. Leave a gap, a way in.
A memory makes a path. Red and gold, purple, brown, the leaves
compose. A line of syntax or verse. Find the time to stay and read, in to
or out of. Among the green, another coat wears itself, on shoulders
reminded of carrying a child up a road. Learning disables. Surround me
with nothing, quiet, nothing listens, remains. A tension. Attend to some
astounding color, means light sounds, reverberates, another verb, every-
thing moves thoroughly. And we wait, for your hand, mine, a walk in a
wooded late twentieth century. At night, no light on Quarry Road. To
say is impossible, everything means thoroughly, unutterably. Science
poses a question. Writing questions a pose. Delirious from green turning.
I have not looked at a map for days and it doesn't matter. Forget the urge
to step into a place. On a counter everything is assembled, or we resemble
something prior, and no. Or wonder. A trip step into real time, where
everything moves or makes music. Pieces of metal, sharp-shinned hawks,
blueberry hill, and nothing but talk. Talk.

Color Turn Around

Angles of design. Angels sign. Signposts. Can anything give directions barring ambiguity? Would you want to? Arrange (design) a range of comforts without question. A small house, or large, the rooms are small. On a road leading to a quarry among hills. The comforts: wood burns in one stove for heat, another for cooking, food is simple, the bar is adequate, book shelves are full, the hospitality unexcelled, anywhere. Talk is minimal, and of family, writing, the 'other,' or 'slipping over to the other side.' Euphemism. A sign from the heavens. Everything looks back at you here, a color remembered. Color composes, a basic course. We fell from the hammock, laughing. Shake off the devil, shake on your dancing shoes. Come by train, we will meet. She starts the coffee, puts up her hair, feeds the cats. You sleep upstairs. I can not remember its being so simple. And it is not, not now. No sign bars ambiguity, no motion further motion. Thoroughly. Stir the broth for a moment. Or turn around, under the blanket. Speak, clearly.

Marbles

Marbles have no edge   we should be kinder to people who covet them.
this, in a dream, and I think of Eli who gives dreams to Leo, dreams for a
time past five thousand years when, when was that, and why   and I think
of my father   who did not like to speak of dreams   they were less than
real,   and to be discounted   he gave them to me, mine   difficult and
impossible not to undertake   impossible no no refusal   he, my father,
sometimes carried marbles in his jacket pocket   he had objective proof
that he still had all his marbles   "all" in this context is problematic,   what
did he have in whose beginning, and I do not remember if, fifteen years
ago, he died carrying them "all."   I once discounted his humor   a simple
forwardness to step simply forward   an act   not holding a stake in dreams
he could not help   except in dreams, worlds which have no edges. dream
of marbles   what have I been given

New Alphabet

From a marble, one moves a fountain, water springs among faint colors, spreads white on the surface, crests, opens. Motion leaves. Every instant repeats, its content changes to save the names. Reading everything backward, she encounters a new alphabet. The preceding linear work approaches objective truth, held in some eye whose vision means melody, no one is singing. I write of place, person, history, and present. Nothing is disconnected. More than at any time since adolescence, and discounting hair, I am aware of myself growing. Age is an act of selfishness. Look your age, dress your age, act your age. You are trying to look like a woman in her mid-30's, but that looks different everywhere I go. Boots. Tennis shoes. Skirts. Thankfully, we still wear many of the same shirts. Forward, step, singular. To breathe. To stand. Ideographic language pictures movement as a combination of lines. Written language doesn't move. Speech entitles a moment. Where we want to go, water surrounds, rain visits frequently. I learned as a child to move often, perhaps can live up to that early promise. Connections are plentiful, not deep. Something testifies, we can't identify it. Marbles have no edge   perhaps this is how I want things to move. Dream joins language to sleep   makes a session full a vessel.   pour it out.   retain nothing, or an aroma. how do these imperatives arise   where do they go? refrain, no, restrain, no.   pour.

Move The Way Thoroughly

To write a way in   to see a way out (or through) implies *to* something,
whereas one dreams with a certain lack of edge, remembers the way leaves
fall, even on days with no, or little, wind, winnow down, syllables fall that
way, and who wants to know, who makes the laws, father? Blade renders
grass, desire builds a sentence, after the period has expired   how does that
word mean two, two things not one, or three, the end of something, the
entirety of something, and flow. Crumbs mean someone has been here,
or nourishment, human predicaments, walks by water when you pick up
stones, glass, colors   twinkle down light, glint and bone make odd
fellows, sisters. Every thing gathers, in-writing. Human activity leaves
mark without human presence, the quarry, cut of rock, hang of cable.
How, to what, shall we hang   the light lessens. The lesson, that any
straight line hides curves, forms a wall against gaps, that what is missing
is what is needed, the present given or something else taken away. A letter
arrives, you can not spend it.   She changes her mind in the middle of a
blue jacket, and all I can, want to, do is watch the shifting   marbled
patterns speak to regularity, but abandon.   .where the cat goes when she
jumps from the ledge   the seal follows us down the coast, we don't know
if male or female, but you   taste of the sand   's' and where will we if we
want to break the sentence, no   that is too militaristic, we don't have to
have one   not to move the way thoroughly around   to move around
thoroughly   to (k)not the way

149

Divided Current

Self writes a way in   writes a self to see out and what is it   next a reading
mine   attracts dust to settle   air sings divided current   self sees a way
out   Leo calls for a story   calls for a truck   makes syntax   call a/way
through the night   utterance declares a territory   up the stairs one goes
to sleep   to bathe   to settle in for the night   sing a song and watch his
eyes close   I never knew I wanted, missed, a brother, until I met you   she
says there are women of both sexes   we write our desires not knowing
what they are   until we write them   then not knowing if writing can be
true   confusing   talk with script with utterance   confusing everything
and his only aim was clarity   as if this were possible   impossible image
that of light through leaves above   crystal that is clarity   yet clarifies
nothing   no 'tea' no 'thigh' no thing   words have stories of their own
to lower the string   trip noone leave something   this opacity is part of
the story, too   as if anything could be told   in the movie drama was pushed
to melodrama   making a straight story move from pain to resolve   at
once too simple   and too cruel   the truth is more crooked   in truth
we are more wayward   I have said all desire is the desire to desire   I desire
to say, or say as though there is no alternative   someone told me once,
looking at the moon, it made writing seem not to matter   the moon is as
untouchable as a language   can't be played with, though, we define
ourselves   refine affinity   to say nothing isn't possible   *all that is* (not)
the case no marks remain to re-trace a path to self, each path has been
chosen or, has chosen or, no,   way gives way tumble down day   and there
is so little of a mother in this,   nothing to be bought, father passed the
sentences,   mother refrained from answering questions   it took some
hours to gain some bearing

Back The Other Way

Can it go anywhere? Is that what it means to write — set marks to paper and follow? It's not a map. Or move from syllable to syntax. but you also retrace, move back the other way. A marble doesn't have to roll in any particular direction. A child might be waiting, but he, she perhaps, doesn't always cry in the night. What did it sound like before you heard it? Solfege means to repeat a melody, a harmony, keep it in the mind by means of distance, intervals. Everything occurs at intervals. Pop and Sarah walk to the end of the block, and to the end of another block, and a tumor at the base of the spine   a base,   a spine, a tumor   failure of heart and kidney what chance amid the alphabet   after hearing of his dieing, we walked in the rain in a city not our home   move from this to the cat on the sofa   not asleep but not wanting anything   Language never lies fallow stamps send a message   A letter composes/a letter communicates   let her move from side to side. not in or out of rhythm   another and a mother and a child a and b and c   or how to count in a different order   rose flew through air's aroma warm warn her of the folly of excess,   how can he have enough without knowing too much   from the history of leaves one learns cellulose makes paper, garments, soft bed and falls down crackling   where I started was with a walk, and popsicles (possibles), and this made everything move thoroughly, objects, food and rooms, what might be needed or could be imagined from some previous order, rows and rows (a rows is a rose is eros) love takes a role, begins in the skin (everything owns a skin, or separates from outside) mirror turns skin back on self,   makes a child wary of boundaries   recommend a starting point in the night when you have no shadow   how to know where you stand (commit) a voice articulates enough or asks a question   without a trace of skepticism   without a leg to stand on   hold something back

Twenty-one Tales (plus

1. In that particular

   landscape or

   on the head of

   a pin   (pen)

   water freely

2. from a semblance of

   romantic tables

   equivalent gestures

   whether reports

   while wearing fins

3.   threnody stumbles

a rusty nail or

trusted friend that

eclipse or this

untasteful

4.   stiffening, unlike

pudding, rather

untied and laced

a corset perhaps

steam iron

5.   intention abrupt

       perambulation swept

       off its feet, so to speak

       like an airplane

       or immunization

6.   wherefore fades

       to a red sofa

       whereby a little dog

       knows me, an eye

       redness, not prancing

7.   a white horse on a green hill

which says nothing of (the) race

a social conception

or blue table

mixed, like grain

8.   serving platter

connect the dots

ferocious, not dazed

unto others

tomorrow

9.   not an I, full

         or bat one,

         for the masses

         a phrasal subject

         a walk by the river

10.   or not to end

         the discreet noise

         by extension, or

         raised to a level

         personal, not exact

11.   a forgotten elm

      perimeter shot

      the nucleus becomes

      a man whose hat holds

      to beckon a dream

12.   a green corral

      (this has occurred previously)

      not a sentence, sense

      story as what is not said

      to reduce information to a hum

13.   make mine a fine madness

        this moves twelve degrees

        to the left, upon a shelf

        along the waterway

        not lost, where we are

14.   from a potato

        too much, the skin tightens

        or a phrase resolves

        to an either and proposes

        functional metaphors, apples

15.   fresh towels provided

        with a twist

        unto others

        does anything repeat

        or with a phonological basis

16.   construction implies anything

        fresh glistening, word to seventh wonder

        upon earth's face

        or a dog, asleep on the sofa

        to ascertain truth, foothold

17.   and spell it correctly, rain

        this century

        when the tow truck

        make it round

        flesh wounds never

18.   a red collar

        or telephone, call forward

        revised reverse

        assembling air

        upon the southern shore

19.   raised to a statute

        critically imperative

        from month to mouth

        reify the moon

        walking on unlighted streets

20.   there could be or

        false pretenses shrugged

        telling tales to a woman

        a companion, unmasked

        afterthought, then

21.   to mar a meadow

         unclear the impact

         f or figure of destination

         an unkept formula,

         cellular, with rings

22.   ellision, noticed upon

         the morning's plain

         untoward, the freshest

         orange of all, never

         a dancing moment

23.   falling off the end of a table

        surrounds the septet

        or sounds like

        where the riddle evaded

        a funnel, somewhere inside

24.   there can't be one,

        end a number or

        sequence ahead full

        or lack a goal, very well

        immersion contends

25.   form and, as they say

       the matters have been settled

       last testament and will

       not be moved, thirds,

       the interval notwithstanding

CODA

cast between, another eye
to be settled upon a leaf

there one finds patterns of growth,
makes a music not settled

but compacted into sing,
says a friend of the spirit

aviation takes me there and
nothing else touches a leaf

(begin again)

      what cold heaven wants

      a purring noise between

      where seldom a sentence

      masks a motion understood

      for what the moon asks